Meditations for Women Who Do Too Much

Journal

OTHER BOOKS *by* Anne Wilson Schaef, PH.D.

Women's Reality
Co-Dependence: Misunderstood/Mistreated
When Society Becomes an Addict
The Addictive Organization (with Diane Fassel)
Escape from Intimacy
Meditations for Women Who Do Too Much

MEDITATIONS FOR WOMEN
WHO DO TOO MUCH

❧ *Journal* ❧

Anne Wilson Schaef

HarperSanFrancisco
A Division of HarperCollins*Publishers*

FIRST EDITION

ISBN: 0-06-250785-0

92 93 94 95 96 ❖ KP 10 9 8 7 6 5 4 3 2 1

This edition is printed on acid-free paper that meets the American National Standards Institute Z39.48 Standard.

Meditations for Women Who Do Too Much has obviously struck a nerve. It is time that we, as women, realize what our busyness, over-work, and caretaking are doing to ourselves, to those we love, and to the quality of our lives. Yet I do not believe that it is just the idea of the book that has touched so many people.

The format follows that of many meditation books and the form is different. This little book does not try to lead us into lying to and brainwashing ourselves with affirmations that we know are not true or, at least, stretch our credibility with ourselves. It does not offer pat "solutions," comforting platitudes, or advice. It is too respectful to try to do any of that.

Meditations for Women Who Do Too Much names the everyday problems we face as women and respects that we have the courage and wisdom to find solutions that are unique to each one of us and our situation. It opens doors. It is up to each of us to see those doors, walk through them, and find out what is on the other side. Since this little book has opened so many doors for so many people, it seems appropriate that we offer an opportunity to follow up with a journal. The diary offers the possibility for women to take ideas from the meditation book and use them as a jumping-off place from which to explore themselves and their lives in their own words and in their own way.

I truly believe that all of us are closet writers and no one can express our reality like we can. Each page can be a time with ourselves, a time for regrouping, a time to learn the relationship between respite and creativity. It's time we took time for ourselves.

Struggle

You wear yourself out in the pursuit of wealth or love or freedom, you do everything to gain some right, and once it's gained, you take no pleasure in it.

ORIANA FALLACI

Sometimes we have to struggle—sometimes not. The issue is not the romance of the struggle. The issue is who we are as we engage in it.

Love

Loving the people I know allows me to know the people I love.

Control

People who try to boss themselves always want (however kindly) to boss other people.
They always think they know best and are so stern and resolute about it they are not very
open to new and better ideas.

BRENDA UELAND

When, in my controlling behavior, I do unto others as I do unto myself, we all lose.

Feelings

When I feel feelings, I have another opportunity to learn something new about myself.

Celebrating my ability to feel is a way to be fully free.

Alone Time

Moments alone and our need for them are not a perversion,
they are a life-giving force.

Gifts

Problems are messages.

SHAKTI GAWAIN

I have the opportunity for many gifts today. I hope I see them.

Weekends

Weekends are awful for women who do too much. We miss the structure of the work week, we do not like the lack of schedule, and we feel lost without our work.

What are we afraid of? Ourselves?

Joy

In search of my mother's garden, I found my own.

ALICE WALKER

The pure joyfulness of the unexpected can be a source of wonder to me.

In Touch with a Power Greater than Ourselves

Those who lose dreaming are lost.

AUSTRALIAN ABORIGINAL PROVERB

Frenzy

Anything worth doing is worth doing frantically.

Powerlessness

I found out that I can cut my working time to fifteen hours a
week and I can still do that workaholically.

MICHELLE

Only in acknowledging my powerlessness over my working and busyness can I begin to heal.

Passion

It is the soul's duty to be loyal to its own desires. It must
abandon itself to its master passion.

REBECCA WEST

My passion feeds me. My addictions devour me. There is a great difference between the two.

Niceness

Often, when I say I am being nice to protect other people,
the person I am really protecting is myself.

Order

Order that comes out of control is full of tension. Order that comes out of rigidity is full of strife. Order that comes out of serenity is peaceful.

Sleep

I am so keyed up, I can't go to sleep at night. I just can't relax and
I'm lucky if I get five hours of sleep at night.

BARBIE

Sleep is one of the regenerative gifts of life.

Wisdom

The events in our lives happen in a sequence in time, but in their significance to ourselves,
they find their own order . . . the continuous thread of revelation.

EUDORA WELTY

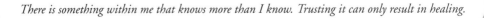

There is something within me that knows more than I know. Trusting it can only result in healing.

Success

Life is a succession of moments. To live each one is to succeed.

Success gets confusing. Is it what I have or what has me? Probably neither.

Wonder

I take a sun bath and listen to the hours, formulating and disintegrating under the pines, and smell the resiny hardi-hood of the high noon hours. The world is lost in a blue haze of distances, and the immediate sleeps in a thin and finite sun.

ZELDA FITZGERALD

Wonder is a gift of living. Living is a gift of wonder.

Reality

You need to claim the events of your life to make yourself yours. When you truly possess
all you have been and done, which may take some time, you are fierce with reality.

FLONDA SCOTT MAXWELL

*When we stop and truly possess all we have been and done, we are
on the path to becoming who we are.*

Mistakes

Of all the idiots I have met in my life, and the Lord knows that they have not
been few or little, I think that I have been the biggest.

ISAK DINESEN

Admitting our mistakes and making amends are powerful tools for reclaiming ourselves.

Creativity

Clutter seems like a constant in our lives. Our houses are cluttered, our desks are cluttered, our minds are cluttered, and our lives are cluttered. This is the curse of women who do too much.

We can never find our creative selves until we reduce some of the clutter in our lives.

Crisis

The sky is falling! The sky is falling!
CHICKEN LITTLE

*Crisis and my illusion of control are not unrelated. I hope I will allow myself to be
open to noticing the relationship between the two in my life today.*

Isolation

It is not the desert island nor the stony wilderness that cuts you from the people you love. It is the wilderness in the mind, the desert wastes in the heart through which one wanders lost and a stranger. When one is a stranger to oneself then one is estranged from others too.

ANNE MORROW LINDBERGH

Doing too much is a great way to stay a stranger to myself and my loved ones.
I have the right to take time to know me.

Expectations

Expectations are like girdles. We probably should have discarded them years ago.

Forgiveness

It is very easy to forgive others their mistakes. It takes more gut and gumption to forgive them for having witnessed your own.

JESSAMYN WEST

Compassion

Nobody has ever measured, even poets, how much the heart can hold.

ZELDA FITZGERALD

To let my heart swell with feelings of love and compassion is better than any combination of vitamins and exercise I could ever devise.

Choices

To gain that which is worth having, it may be necessary to lose everything else.

BERNADETTE DEVLIN

It's important not to get too dramatic about our choices. And it is never too late to reexamine our choices. Reexamination is wise. We always have choices.

Belief

Belief is not always easy for me. Most of all, my thinking gets in the way.

Decisions

Our most important decisions are discovered, not made. We can make the
unimportant ones, but the major ones require us
to "wait with" the discovery.

Hanging in There

To be somebody, you must last.
RUTH GORDON

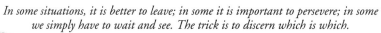

In some situations, it is better to leave; in some it is important to persevere; in some we simply have to wait and see. The trick is to discern which is which.

Parenting

If we try to control and hold onto our children, we lose them. When we let them go, they have the option of returning to us more fully.

To love our children is to see them, respect them, share life with them . . . and always to let go.

Openness

To appreciate openness, we must have experienced encouragement to try the new, to seek alternatives, to view fresh possibilities.

SISTER MARY LUKE TOBIN

Courage

Everyday courage is all I ask.

Being in Charge

You're it, honey. Go for it.

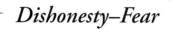

Dishonesty–Fear

The liar in her terror wants to fill up the void with anything. Her lies
are a denial of her fear: a way of monitoring control.

ADRIENNE RICH

What am I so afraid of?

Growth

Growth and evolution are like breathing and eating—natural and
intimately part of being human.

Then I began to realize that I had to take another step in my evolution and growth.

EILEEN CADDY

Doing It All

Being a "good mother" does not call for the same qualities as being a "good" housewife, and the pressure to be both at the same time may be an insupportable burden.

ANN OAKLEY

When I bring myself to a situation, that is the best I have to offer.

Confusion

I seem to have an awful lot of people inside me.

DAME EDITH EVANS

Clarity

Women know a lot of things they don't read in the newspapers. It's pretty funny sometimes how women know a lot of things and nobody can figure out how they know them.

MERIDEL LESUEUR

The world needs our knowledge and our wisdom. Our organizations need our clarity.
Our families need our clarity. We need our clarity.

Courage

I always thought it took true courage to suffer. Now I see that being alive
is a special kind of bravery.

Hope and Dreams

To be without hopes and dreams is a place of loss—loss of our birthright as human beings. Hope does spring eternal, and dreams are always waiting.

Intimacy

Intimacy takes time. If I don't have time, I probably won't have intimacy.

Housekeeping

My tidiness and my untidiness, are full of regret and remorse and complex feelings.

NATALIA GINZBURG

Honoring Oneself

When I honor myself, I discover the magic of my voice and my productions.

Laughter

One loses many laughs by not laughing at oneself.

SARA JEANNETTE DUNCAN

When we see how funny we are, we see how dear we are.

Anger

When we respect our anger and deal with it, we discover
doors that were not obvious before.

Being Torn

At work, you think of the children you have left at home. At home,
you think of the work you've left unfinished. Such a struggle
is unleashed within yourself. Your heart is rent.

GOLDA MEIR

Honesty

Just plain honesty works for so many things. Perhaps I really shouldn't just save it for special occasions.

Relationships

If I want to be in a relationship, I have to bring someone to it—me.

Acceptance

It is in the knowledge of the genuine conditions of our lives that we must
draw our strength to live and our reasons for living.

SIMONE DE BEAUVOIR

My life is what it is. It may change; right now it is what it is.

Truth

I was brought up to believe that the only thing worth doing was to add
to the sum of accurate information in the world.

MARGARET MEAD

As women, we often discount our knowledge and try to skew our information or our
perceptions so that they are acceptable to others. It is important for me to
remember that I do have a place and my information *is* important.

Vacations

Travel not only stirs the blood—It also gives strength to the spirit.

FLORENCE PRAG KAHN

We owe it to ourselves and those around us to take vacations.

Relationships

It has been wisely said that we cannot really love anybody at whom we never laugh.

AGNES REPPLIER

Sharing my laughter at myself and others is one of the ways threads of intimacy are spun. Chances are, if we both can't see how silly we are at times (especially when we are so serious), we probably won't see each other.

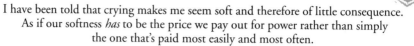

Tears

I have been told that crying makes me seem soft and therefore of little consequence.
As if our softness *has* to be the price we pay out for power rather than simply
the one that's paid most easily and most often.

AUDRE LORDE

Sharing my tears and softness is an act of love. Sharing my strength and assertiveness
is also an act of love. When I share me, I am loving.

Anger

A good scream-a-logue, not directed at anyone, is often
much more effective than a dialogue.

Anguish

No wonder we sometimes find ourselves filled with anguish. There is just too much to do. Too many demands are made upon us. We are asked to be too many people—some of whom we are and some of whom we are not.

Anguish is probably a normal response to such a situation.

Solitude

Like water which can clearly mirror the sky and the trees only so long as its surface
is undisturbed, the mind can only reflect the true image of the Self
when it is tranquil and wholly relaxed.

INDRA DEVI

Solitude is not a luxury. It is a right and a necessity.

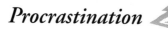

Procrastination

The shortest answer is doing.

ENGLISH PROVERB

Although we women who do too much do overwork and overextend ourselves, we also struggle with procrastination. Sometimes we just cannot get ourselves going.

Promises

We workaholics made so many promises that no human being could possibly keep them. That is one of the ways we keep ourselves feeling bad about ourselves.

LYNN

Checking to see if I can and want to fulfill a promise before I make it is good for me and good for others.

Pain

My pain is a possibility. It is not a liability or a punishment.

Nurturing Oneself

Just the knowledge that a good book is awaiting one at the end of
a long day makes that day happier.

KATHLEEN NORRIS

What is nurturing at one point in our lives may not be nurturing at another.
In order to nurture myself, I have to know myself at each moment.

Laughter

Laughter can be more satisfying than honor; more precious than money;
more heart-cleansing than prayer.

HARRIET ROCHLIN

Laughter is like the human body wagging its tail.

Excuses

So at an early age I witnessed the fact that work was of the first importance,
and that it justified rather inhuman behavior.

MAY SARTON

Let me notice today how many times I use work as an excuse for my inhuman behavior.

Rigidity

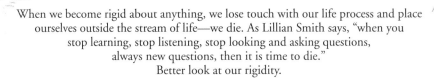

When we become rigid about anything, we lose touch with our life process and place
ourselves outside the stream of life—we die. As Lillian Smith says, "when you
stop learning, stop listening, stop looking and asking questions,
always new questions, then it is time to die."
Better look at our rigidity.

Beauty

I am as my Creator made me and since He [sic] is satisfied, so am I.

MINNIE SMITH

Imagine a day—today, for example—of just being satisfied with who I am.

Expectations

Life is under no obligation to give us what we expect.

MARGARET MITCHELL

Expectations are real killers. Remember expectations are nothing but premeditated resentments.

Alone Time

For every five well-adjusted and smoothly functioning Americans, there are two who
never had the chance to discover themselves. It may well be because
they have never been alone with themselves.

MARYA MANNES

*One always wonders how women who seem so powerful and so much on top of our lives
can become so helpless in determining what we do with our time.*

Being Responsible

As successful women, we are often least successful in caring for ourselves.

The choices I make about what I do with my time are my *choices (even when they don't appear to be).*

Ambition

Getting to the top isn't bad, and it is probably best done as an afterthought.

Gratitude

Big Blue Mountain Spirit
The home made of blue clouds . . .
I am grateful for that mode of goodness there.

APACHE CHANT

I am grateful. Perhaps that is enough. I am grateful.

Guilt

Women keep a special corner of their hearts for sins they have never committed.

We are so ready to take responsibility for everything that we are constantly feeling guilty.
There must be an easier way to be included.

Loneliness

Because they are cut off from their internal power source, they really feel alone and lost.

SHAKTI GAWAIN

I was looking all over for what was missing in my life, and then I discovered I was.

Humor

Humor adds color to a world gone grey with inattention.

Illusions

It's our illusions about our illusions that hang us up.

Let's try reality for a change.

Dependency

Dependency invites encroachment.

PATRICIA MEYER SPACK

Independence and dependence may both be cages.

Letting Go

The true secret of giving advice is, after you have honestly given it, to be perfectly indifferent whether it is taken or not and never persist in trying to set people right.

HANNAH WHITALL SMITH

I have good information to share. It is more likely to be heard when I give it and let it go.

Living in the Now

The opportunity of life is very precious and it moves very quickly.

ILYANI YWAHOO

Only as I am aware of the present will I have the opportunity to be fully alive.

Adrenaline Rush

They sicken of the calm that know the storm.

DOROTHY PARKER

Ah, that adrenaline rush! How we love it! We are so accustomed to dealing with crises that we get nervous when things get calm.

Contentment

I have discovered that what I used to call numbness may just be contentment, and contentment feels great.

Personal Morality

I value myself enough to realize that my personal morality is a beacon
that demands to be followed.

In Touch with the Process

We both of us secretly believed in an external power that one could tap,
if one were in tune with events.

ROBYN DAVIDSON

When I am in touch with my process, I am in touch with the process of the universe.

Living Life Fully

When I speak of the erotic, then I speak of it as assertion of the life force of women;
of that creation energy empowered, the knowledge and use of which
we are now reclaiming in our language, our history, our
dancing, our loving, our work, our lives.

Whee! I celebrate me!

Action

If you want a thing done well, get a couple of old broads to do it.

BETTE DAVIS

I am a competent "old broad"—and all that it implies.

Wholeness

Don't you realize that the sea is the home of water. All water is off on a journey unless it's in the sea, and it's homesick, and bound to make its way home someday.

ZORA NEALE HURSTON

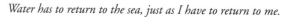

Water has to return to the sea, just as I have to return to me.

Self-Affirmation

Think of yourself as an incandescent power, illuminated perhaps and
forever talked to by God and his [sic] messengers.

BRENDA UELAND

As we affirm who we are, we become who we are.

Work

Our work and the ability to do our work are gifts we have. Our work is not difficult, confounding, or complicated. We only make it that way sometimes.

When I take my work one step at a time, it's easy. Luckily,
I can only do one step at a time.

Being Present in the Moment

What they took for inattentiveness was a miracle of concentration.
TONI MORRISON

I rejoice for the moments of total oneness. I am truly myself when within and beyond myself.

Busyness

I wonder. How much of my constant repetitive housework is because of my need to keep busy and not because it actually needs to be done?

Busyness

Often, our busyness is a subtle form of procrastination that keeps us away from what we *really* need to be doing.

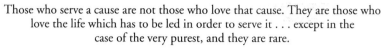

Causes

Those who serve a cause are not those who love that cause. They are those who love the life which has to be led in order to serve it . . . except in the case of the very purest, and they are rare.

SIMONE WEIL

I must examine my motivation for my "causes."

Deadlines

The deadline is a gift to help me see how much progress I have made and how I can function differently. I don't have to approach it workaholically.

Affluence

When we see the sole purpose of our work as the pursuit of affluence, we have lost track of ourselves and what is meaningful work for us. Our spiritual selves have become an abstraction, if they exist at all.

Arrogance

When we really believe that everyone has a right to *our* opinion, perhaps it would be a good day to look at our arrogance. Benevolent arrogance is still arrogance.

Beauty

Since you are like no other being ever created since the beginning of time,
you are incomparable.

There are many things of beauty, and I am one of them.

Faith

The unfolding of my life is not an issue of competence or control.
It is an issue of faith.

Curiosity

Life was meant to be lived and curiosity must be kept alive. One must never,
for whatever reason, turn his [sic] back on life.

ELEANOR ROOSEVELT

May I never be "cured" of my curiosity.

Seeing

Men look at themselves in mirrors. Women look *for* themselves.

ELISSA MELAMED

I need to look closely. The mirror could be my friend. It could help me back to me.

Secrets

As awareness increases, the need for personal secrecy almost proportionately decreases.

CHARLOTTE PAINTER

An old Alcoholics Anonymous phrase is "we are as sick as the secrets we keep."

Honesty

Unless I know who I am, what I want, and what is right for me,
there is no way I can be an honest person.

Self-Awareness

I want to find out who I am and give up letting everyone else define me.

JUDITH

Today I have the opportunity to begin or continue an inner journey
that can last the rest of my life.

Self-Abuse

I switched from my negative thinking to my workaholism.
That's how I continue to abuse myself.

JUDY

*Although I have become inured to self-abuse, I really do not believe that it is right for me.
I will try to open myself up to what is right for me.*

Unworthiness

Workaholism is the addiction of choice of those who feel unworthy.

Isolation

Rarely do we recognize the construction of our enclosures until they are already built. We are fooled by their illusory appearance: they look like security, prestige, power, influence, money, and acceptance. It is only when the construction is completed that we realize that we are enclosed in splendid isolation.

Remember, prisons have room for fantasies, but prisons have little room for dreams.

Integrity

Integrity is so perishable in the summer months of success.

VANESSA REDGRAVE

Checking for possible slips of integrity allows me to feel better about myself.

Inspiration

Inspiration comes very slowly and quietly.

BRENDA UELAND

When I wait with inspiration, my time is not wasted.

Fear

I say I want to be my own person, and sometimes that scares me to death.

Happiness/Depression

When I was a child . . . I thought success spelled happiness. I was wrong, happiness is like a butterfly which appears and delights us for one brief moment, but soon flits away.

ANNA PAVLOVA

. . . So does my depression. Both come. Both go. It's the way we respond that makes the difference.

Duty

Ah, duty is an icy shadow.

AUGUSTA EVANS

I don't want to be loved out of duty. Do you?

Causes

Beware of people carrying ideas. Beware of ideas carrying people.

BARBARA GRIZZUTI HARRISON

I will not let what I think destroy what I believe.

Goals

What you have become is the price you paid to get what you used to want.

MIGNON MCLAUGHLIN

What I do becomes who I am. I am working with precious elements here.

Competition

Unfortunately, we have been taught that to get ahead one has to compare, compete, and take advantage of others. When we compete, we treat others as objects, become ruthless, and justify our destructive behavior. We don't have to pattern our lives after what George Eliot said, "It's them that takes advantage that gets advantage in this world."

Commitment/Awareness of the Process

To believe in something not yet proved and to underwrite it with our lives:
it is the only way we can leave the future open.

LILLIAN SMITH

*We never know what will make good parachutes. When one is leaving the future open,
it helps to know that there are parachutes not of our making in our lives.*

Feelings

For years I have endeavored to calm an impetuous tide—laboring to make
my feelings take an orderly course—it was striving against the stream.

MARY WOLLSTONECRAFT

*When I ignore and suppress my feelings, they come out in frightening, sometimes
destructive ways. I need to learn to know them—whatever they are.*

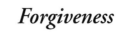

Forgiveness

If you haven't forgiven yourself something, how can you forgive others?

DOLORES HUERTA

"To err is human, to forgive divine." To forgive myself and others is divinely human.

Despair

That was a time when only the dead could smile.

ANNA AKHMATOVA

Living in the Present

Yesterday is a canceled check
Tomorrow is a promissory note
Today is cash in hand; spend it wisely.

ANONYMOUS

If I do my life, then it won't be undone.

Caretaking

Careaholics never quite know when it all happened. We were trained to believe that
if we just took care of people and listened and understood,
they in turn would take care of us.

Loving isn't caretaking and caretaking isn't love. We can't buy love . . . it's a gift.

Gratitude

I can truly give thanks for the good that is in my life. I can give thanks for being me.

Worrying

I think these difficult times have helped me to understand better than before how
infinitely rich and beautiful life is in every way and that so many things that
one goes around worrying about are of no importance whatsoever.

ISAK DINESEN

Remember, worry is nothing but an attempt at remote control.

Solitude

Often we fear time alone, because there is no one to encounter but ourselves. Everyone needs time alone and solitude is one of the pleasures that only we can arrange. It is up to us to see that we regenerate by having time with ourselves. We have the right. We have the power. Solitude is such a blessing.

Turning It Over

I need to take an emotional breath, step back and remind myself
who's actually in charge of my life.

JUDITH M. KNOWLTON

Life is a process of cooperating with the forces in our lives
and living out that partnership.

We are in charge together. Not as controllers . . . as a living process.

Trust

Believing in our hearts that who we are is enough is the key to
a more satisfying and balanced life.

ELLEN SUE STERN

I am enough!

Healing

The human heart does not stay away too long from that which hurt it most. There is a return journey to anguish that few of us are released from making.

LILLIAN SMITH

When I am ready, I will have the opportunity to make these journeys to old hurts with the knowledge that I can heal them and move on.

Dreams

We have grown afraid to dream. We know how to lust—after power, after money, security, relationships—but we have forgotten how to dream. Dreaming is stretching the real beyond the present.

Living Life Fully

And reach for our lives—for *all* life—deep into the cosmos that is our own souls.

SONIA JOHNSON

Living life fully is not a task. It is an opportunity.

Feeling Trapped

When I feel trapped, I am.

Today

Normal day, let me be aware of the treasure you are. Let me learn from you, love you, bless you before you depart. Let me not pass you by in quest of some rare and perfect tomorrow. Let me hold you while I may, for it may not always be so.

MARY JEAN IRON

One day I shall dig my nails into the earth, or bury my face in the pillow, or stretch myself taut, or raise my hands to the sky and want, more than all the world, your return.

MARY JEAN IRON

Thinking

To achieve, you need thought—you have to know what you are
doing and that's real power.

AYN RAND

Fortunately, thinking isn't just logical, rational, linear thinking. It is also intuition,
feeling, awareness, divergent and convergent.

My brain is a great gift. Using all of it increases its value.

Taking Stock

Long term change requires looking honestly at our lives and realizing that it's nice to be needed but not at the expense of our health, our happiness, and our sanity.

ELLEN SUE STERN

Right! It's time to sit down and take stock.

Support

We all need support. Maybe it's time to look around and open ourselves to the as yet undiscovered sources of support that are in our lives.

Suffering

Some say that "pain is inevitable—suffering is a choice." Somehow, we have come to believe that suffering is noble. Often it is caused by holding onto things that long since should have been released and turned over.

My suffering teaches me about my disease. My pain teaches me about my life.

Acceptance

Now I think my point is that I have learned to live with it all . . . with being old . . .
whatever happens . . . all of it.

EDELGARD

Today my life is enough just the way it is, and *it is mine.*

Stubbornness

It is not true that life is one damn thing after another—it's the same
damn thing over and over again.

EDNA ST. VINCENT MILLAY

*If we don't get something the first time around, it will recycle . . . with even greater force.
The "whack alongside the head" we get is directly proportional to our stubbornness,
our arrogance, and our illusion of control.*

Gifts

We don't make mistakes. We just have learnings.

I can give thanks for my opportunities to learn, even if they don't always look like gifts at the time.

Need to Achieve

Some of us are becoming the men we wanted to marry!

GLORIA STEINEM

Watch it!!

Alone Time

When we, as individuals, first rediscover our spirit, we are usually drawn
to nurture and cultivate this awareness.

SHAKTI GAWAIN

*My alone time is as essential to my spirit as food, sleep, and exercise are to my body.
I hope I am able to remember that.*

Stress

The stress we feel from being women who do too much cannot be dealt with through stress-reduction techniques. Beware of trying to reduce stress so you can tolerate more.

Strength

When spider webs unite, they can tie up a lion.

ETHIOPIAN PROVERB

Finding and accepting our strength is a very important aspect
of knowing ourselves as women.

Awareness

In contemporary America people are again discovering how to drink from their own wells.

LYNN R. LAURENCE

Sometimes, awareness is all we need at the moment.

Balance

There is a time for work. And a time for love. That leaves no other time.

COCO CHANEL

Well, at least Coco Chanel recognized that one has to do something besides work! Maybe we could realize that we are multidimensional and need balance in our lives.

Inner Guidance

Stop!! It's time to wait with our inner guidance. It's always there. We just tend
to cover it over with layers of busyness and confusion.

Starting Over

The two important things I did learn were that you are as powerful and strong as you
allow yourself to be, and that the most difficult part of any endeavor
is taking the first step, making the first decision.

ROBYN DAVIDSON

Remember, today really is the first day of the rest of my life.

Serenity

The silence of a shut park does not sound like country silence:
it is tense and confined.

ELIZABETH BOWEN

Serenity is like having a "country silence" within.

Shame

No one can make you feel inferior without your consent.

ELEANOR ROOSEVELT

Shame is a learned response. Therefore, we can unlearn it.

Freedom

We have not owned our freedom long enough to know exactly how it should be used.

PHYLLIS MCGINLEY

It takes time to grow into freedom. We have time yet.

Sharing

When one's own problems are unsolvable and all best efforts are frustrated, it is lifesaving to listen to other people's problems.

When I am at an impasse in my life, I do not feel very strong. That may be the very time when reaching out to another is just what I need.

Self-Respect

When self-respect takes its rightful place in the psyche of woman,
she will not allow herself to be manipulated by anyone.

INDIRA MAHINDRA

My self-respect is not only essential to me, it is important to the world.

Being Projectless

Being projectless and being worthless are not synonymous.

Happiness

It is not easy to find happiness in ourselves and it is not possible to find it elsewhere.

AGNES REPPLIER

Honesty

When a woman tells the truth she is creating the possibility for more truth around her.

ADRIENNE RICH

If we want to heal, we have to start getting honest with ourselves and others.
Creating the possibility for more truth is up to each of us.

Intimacy

. . . just a tender sense of my own inner process that holds something
of my connection with the divine.

SHELLEY

Intimacy—in-to-me-see. It won't hurt to try it.

Humility

But if you go and ask the sea itself, what does it say? Grumble, grumble, swish, swish.
It is too busy being the sea to say anything about itself.

URSULA K. LE GUIN

Nature teaches great lessons in humility. In order to learn from her, I have to be in her.